Musical
Improvisation
For Children

Part of the Creative Ability
Development Series

by Alice Kay Kanack

Cover Art: Mary Cavallo Greve

© 1998 Summy-Birchard Music
division of Summy-Birchard Inc.

Summy-Birchard Inc.
exclusively distributed by
Warner Bros. Publications
15800 NW 48th Avenue
Miami, Florida 33014
All Rights Reserved

This book is dedicated to
Elena Titakis
and
Joey Trout
without whom it might never have
been written

Table of Contents

Introduction

This book is intended to revolutionize the development of creativity in all children by teaching parents the correct way to guide them.

By two years of age, all children are miniature artists. They attempt to communicate (through drawing, singing, play-acting, etc.) their highest aesthetic ideals. They do so in an uninhibited and often rough fashion. By the age of five or six that beautiful expressive freedom has often been unwittingly destroyed by brothers, sisters, parents and teachers. It is one of the goals of this method and this book to teach parents how to control the creative environment of their child, so that his innate creative ability can remain uninhibited and can develop in a natural way.

The second goal of this book is to stimulate the growth and development of the creative part of the brain. Through games and exercises designed just for the enormous imagination (and physical limitations) of the two-to five-year-old*, a child can greatly heighten and develop his natural creative ability.

What You Will Need

#1 - A compact disc player with speakers of some kind (no headphones).

#2 - A well-tuned piano or synthesized keyboard.

An acoustic piano is the preferred instrument, but recognizing that not everyone has one at their disposal, I designed the exercises so that they could be used with any keyboard as long as it is tuned to H=440. In other words, if the instructions call for the use of white keys only, the sounds the keyboard makes should match the recording. (Any good quality synthesizer should do this.)

* Although this book was written with two-to five-year-olds in mind, it actually serves as an excellent introduction to creative musical expression at any age.

Creative Ability Development (CAD) Philosophy

CAD is not about how to play an instrument; it's about how to use the instrument to be an artist.

Every child is an artist.
Every child is unique.
Every child is born with creative ability.
Every child can develop it.

CAD is about going deep inside yourself, discovering your uniqueness, and expressing it.

CAD teaches respect for the ideas of others. Creativity is built on creativity.
Every new idea presented to a child is absorbed, internalized and recreated by him.

CAD is each child's personal search for truth and beauty within himself and the world around him.

The Formula

Freedom of Choice

+

Disciplined Practice

=

The Development of Creative Ability

How to Use this Book

The secret of the development of creative ability is actually an incredibly simple formula:

Freedom of Choice
(i.e. freedom from criticism)
+
Disciplined Practice
(repetition of a creative exercise)
=
The Development of Creative Ability

To practice this formula with the CAD method:

#1 -   Put on the recording.

#2 -   Allow the child to play anything
he wants with it.

Do not criticize, correct, suggest or
shape his ideas in any way.

#3 -   Repeat the same exercise daily
for 1-2 weeks.

#4 -   Repeat the above with a new exercise.
(Review the old exercises periodically.)

The Creative Process Theory

1. Conscious Work

2. Subconscious Work

3. Inspiration

4. Theory

How It Works
The Creative Process Theory

The creative process is a four-part series of events which occur in the brain.

Part One - Conscious Work: The conscious part of the brain attempts to find a solution to a given problem. (In this case, a melody which fits with the given harmony or accompaniment. The possibilities are endless and there is actually no wrong solution possible. Repetition of this creative search is the key to the entire creative process.)

Part Two - Subconscious Work: Triggered by the conscious repetition of a creative exercise, the creative subconscious takes over the problem and attempts to solve it while the conscious part of the brain is resting. This part of the brain evidently works at an extremely heightened level, but only if triggered by the conscious repetition of the creative exercise.

Part Three - Inspiration: When the subconscious has reached a solution to the given problem, it presents this solution to the conscious in the form of an inspiration. An inspiration always occurs in a completed state (i.e., listening to a recording). It can occur during a creative exercise, or in between practices.

Part Four - Theory: In order to understand the inspiration, theory is often used. Understanding inspirations can lead to the entire creative process repeating on a higher level.

(Note: Between the ages of two and five, theory is not necessary and would actually interfere with the child's natural creative freedom. Therefore, any necessary theory is introduced in the simplest of ways, i.e. "Play only on the white keys" instead of "Play in the key of C major." You will find I do name and teach the identification of several modes and keys within this program, so that the student can name what his ear is learning to identify. It is similar to naming the colors of crayons.)

The Three Rules

#1 - "There's No Such Thing as a mistake."

#2 - "Applause and silence."

#3 - "Never Criticize a Friend."

How to Instill Confidence in Self-Expression, Creativity and Self-Criticism

In teaching CAD for over ten years to classrooms of children, I discovered the secret to instilling confidence in self-expression, creativity, and self-criticism. I present this secret in the form of three rules at the first class and repeat them whenever necessary.

#1 - "There's No Such Thing as a Mistake"

The creative process is each individual's search for his own unique solution to a given problem. There is no right or wrong solution; only a choice of what each individual likes or doesn't like. Any person who criticizes becomes the creator by virtue of his criticism, because the solution becomes what the criticizer likes and not what the creator likes. Therefore - NO criticism is allowed!

> No Suggestions
> No Corrections
> No Interruptions

#2 - "Applause and Silence"

Silence: Silence means "absolute attention!" Listen when your child is playing. Children have a very strong need to communicate to you. Don't ever ignore them.

NEVER: Daydream while they're playing.
Do something else while they're playing.
Talk to someone while they're playing.
Answer the phone while they're playing.

Applause: Applause means applaud when your child has finished. Always respond in a positive manner. Say how it made you feel, what images it presented to you, or how proud you are of your child for his amazing ability to create music.

#3 - "Never Criticize a Friend"

For the same reason as the #1 rule, no one must be allowed to criticize the creator. There may often be more than one person in the room when a child is creating. Those people must obey rules #1, #2 and #3 as well. In this way, you can control the environment of your child completely. This is very important because children are very aware of everyone in the room and will try to communicate with everyone.

Children taking turns in this environment will learn the art of listening which has a great deal to do with the development of ideas as well as the development of respect for each other's creative abilities.

Getting Started

It is sometimes difficult to get a two-to five-year-old to do something we want him to do. It is in the nature of a child this age to resist an adult's suggestion in order to demonstrate his independence. It is important not to fight this natural part of a child's growth, but rather to work within it; to understand it and approach the task at hand with wisdom and ingenuity. The following steps will help make your work easier.

Step One - Preparation:

Listen to the recording.
Dance to the recording.
Draw pictures to the recording.
Talk about the music. (What do you hear? What does it sound like?)

Step Two - Demonstrate:

Put on the recording and do the exercise yourself in your child's presence. (Children love to imitate adults.) Be sure to follow the instructions so that what you do does not appear too complicated.

Step Three - Explain the rules:

Tell your child that you are making up some music. Explain that when someone does this "There's no such thing as a mistake!" It's kind of like choosing colors when you color a picture, you just pick ones you like. Only in music you pick notes you like. In the beginning you just have to try them all to find which ones you like. (If there is anyone else in the room be sure the other two rules are discussed.)

Step Four - Invite your child to play:

If your child is two or three and likes to be picked up, simply place him on your lap at the key board as you play. Invite him to join you. (He may wish to play alone, which of course you allow him to do).

If your child is older, simply invite him to join you as you play, or to play by himself if he wishes.

Step Five - Invite your child to take turns:

If your child is only playing when you do, suggest taking turns. Explain that you can each use more of the notes that way. Be sure to listen while he plays and applaud after.

Step Six - Games:

A great way to get a reticent child involved is through the use of games. Get a group of children or siblings together and try some of the games at the end of the book. Be sure all three rules are discussed in the language of the children before beginning.

For Example:

#1 -   "There's No Such Thing as a Mistake." No matter what you play you can't make a mistake, because you're making it up.

#2 -   "Applause and Silence" - Be quiet when someone is playing and clap when they're finished. This is respectful and polite. Also, it's hard to concentrate if someone is making noise while you're playing.

#3 -   "Never Criticize a Friend" - We're all friends and because "There's no such thing as a mistake," nobody can tell anybody what to do. Nobody can say someone did something wrong.

Don't worry if the initial attempts to interest your child fail.
    Don't push!
    Don't rush!

Wait until your child is ready. Do more preparation (step one). Be patient. Often children need to bathe in the music for a while before they're ready to begin. Do the exercises yourself daily.

Don't worry if your child only wants to play for a few seconds. This is normal. Let the child stop when he wants. Let him continue if he wants. The child must be the leader.

Physical Technique

Fine motor skills are often not yet developed in two-to five-year-olds. It is therefore important to provide easier physical steps to match each child's normal growth and development. They are as follows:

Step #1:   Banging - This is the way most children begin to play the piano. It is the most natural. Encourage the child to use his fists, palms, all fingers, elbows etc. In other words, anything goes as long as it's easy and comfortable.

Step #2:   One Finger Hopping - Make the hand into a fist, and then stick out the pointer (first) finger. Use this finger to hop from key to key. This is a transition from banging to fine motor control. It allows a child to create single note melodies before he is able to use all his fingers individually.

Step #3:   Walking Fingers - Alternate individual fingers and thumbs on individual keys. This is actually the way the piano is played most of the time, but it is the most difficult for young children.

The music for the exercises is designed to follow these three steps. Students will probably need to alternate between steps one and two for a while, and then between steps two and three until they are comfortable with each.

A Word About Technique

In the beginning, comfort is more important than technique. Allow your child to:
> Stand and play,
> sit on your lap and play,
> or sit in a chair and play.
> Be aware of his comfort!

Don't worry that your child will develop bad habits that will hamper his ability to play the piano later in life; he won't – creative expression is the most natural, organic, physically relaxing way to start to play an instrument. Music comes directly from the heart and mind into the fingers freely, without inhibitions, without tensions. Any artist or teacher will agree that this is the ultimate goal of every musician's technique. In over ten years of experimental research, CAD has proven to greatly facilitate a student's technical development.

While this is true, technique is not, and has never been, the point of CAD. Any mention or focus on technique during a creative exercise will hamper the student's creative process. Therefore, when the child is ready, provide him with private piano lessons, separate from CAD in order to learn technique and repertoire.

What the Practice of CAD Can Do for a Child

The Development of a Unique Musicality

When a child learns to play an instrument the initial focus is always on the technical aspects of mastering the instrument. (i.e. proper body and hand positions, posture, correct notes to play, learning how to play quickly, accurately and in a coordinated fashion, etc.) While CAD can aid in the development of these skills, that is <u>not</u> its purpose or goal. CAD is not about how to play an instrument, it's about how to use the instrument to be an artist.

An artist is someone who can express his own unique ideas or truths in an aesthetically beautiful and powerful way. In the language of music, an artist is defined as one who is extremely proficient technically as well as one who possesses the deep, unique expressive capability known as musicality.

CAD deals with the musical aspects of playing; in traditional methods of teaching, musicality is almost always taught through imitation (i.e. the student is instructed to play like the teacher, or like the artist in a recording). This does not develop the student's own expression because it is the imitation of someone else's feelings and ideas.

CAD goes directly to each child's own feelings and ideas, therefore it draws out each child's own unique personality. Through repetition of the creative exercises, this unique expression develops, grows confident, becomes defined, and can be transferred to any language a child chooses to use. For example, after studying CAD even for a short period of time, the child will begin to demonstrate a unique musicality in his study of regular repertoire; particularly if he is asked to play the music as if he wrote it himself.

It is an incredibly exciting and moving experience to watch your child's unique personality coming forth in a creative musical expression. All children develop this ability by the end of the first three years of CAD study. Be patient during this time by remembering:

1 - Every child is unique: It is that wonderful uniqueness that will come out in his playing.

2 - Every child is born with creative ability: It is part of the natural function of the brain.

3 - Every child can develop his innate creative ability to a high level: It simply takes a great deal of repetition of creative exercises, in an environment free from criticism, and the time necessary for growth and development.

The Development of an Artistic Character

The character of an artist is one in which a person strives to express his highest ideals of truth and beauty to the world around him. He has respect for the ideas of others, knowing that all creativity is built on creativity. Also, creativity is the opposite of destruction.

When a child practices the art of creativity he is searching for his best solution to a given problem (which is the search for beauty); he is searching for his own unique and most honest solution (which is the search for truth); and he is listening without criticism to the ideas of others (which is respect for the ideas of others). Therefore, through the daily practice of CAD a child learns in the most natural, organic way, what it is to be an artist at the highest level. He feels, expresses and communicates truth, beauty and a deep sensitivity to those around him.

This is the ultimate goal of CAD!

SPECIFIC INSTRUCTIONS

Part One
Legends, Fairy Tales and Images

The initial set of exercises serves a dual purpose: One, to stimulate a child's first musical ideas through images, stories, and imaginative music; and two, to simplify the beginning physical technique through music which suggests the use of palms, fists or bunches of fingers.

Each of these pieces is played exclusively on the white keys or exclusively on the black keys as specified in each exercise. In general it's a good idea to place the child on the upper (or right hand) side of the keyboard. This helps him to play more easily with the harmonic structures of the pieces. He may of course use any part of the keyboard he wishes to. The child may also use fists, palms, bunches of fingers or single fingers as he desires in these first exercises. Encourage your child to play any way he wishes. Remind him often that "THERE'S NO SUCH THING AS A MISTAKE!"

Each of these exercises may be prepared in the following ways:
Listen to the music.
Dance to the music.
Draw to the music.
Talk about the music.

Thunderstorm

Things to Listen For:

>   Thunder
>   Clouds
>   Hail
>   Rain
>   Sunshine
>   Rainbows

Listen also for the song:

It's rain - ing it's pour - ing the old man is snor - ing, he went to bed and he bumped his head and he could-n't get up in the morn - ing.

Playing instructions:

>   Use only the white keys.
>   Play any way you want to.

Fairies

Listen for:

>   Fairies
>   Are they hopping?
>   dancing?
>   flying?

Playing instructions:

>   Play only on the black keys.
>   Play any way you want to.
>   Play anything you want to.

Stars and Moons

Listen for:

      Round shapes - (the moon)

      Sparkling sounds - (the stars)

Playing instructions:

      Play only on the white keys.

      Play any way you want to.

      Play anything you want to.

Rainbows

Listen for:

      Rainbows

      Rain

      Sun

Playing instructions:

      Play only on the black keys.

      Play any way you want to.

      Play anything you want to.

Pegasus

Begin this exercise by telling the story of Pegasus and Bellerophon as written here.

The Story

Long ago, according to legends, there lived a magical horse named Pegasus. Pegasus was a beautiful white horse with wings. He was wild and free, and flew through the sky and galloped on the ground.

At the same time in history, there lived a great hero by the name of Bellerophon. One day, as Bellerophon was sleeping, he had a dream. In the dream, a goddess named Minerva told him that he could capture Pegasus and ride the great horse.

Bellerophon woke up and found a golden bridle beside him. Bellerophon chased Pegasus and using the golden bridle was able to leap on his back and ride him. Knowing that he was riding a great and noble horse, Bellerophon decided to do battle with the terrible monster Chimeara who was terrorizing the kingdom.

With great strength and bravery, Bellerophon and Pegasus swept down from the sky to the terrible monster. There was a great battle, for the monster was very strong, but in the end Pegasus and Bellerophon won. The monster was destroyed.

After that, Pegasus and Bellerophon became great friends and flew around the world protecting the good people in all the kingdoms. They were loved and respected by all the people.

One day Bellerophon, who thought by this time that he could do anything, decided he would ride Pegasus towards the sun and visit the gods on Mount Olympus. So he and Pegasus flew higher and higher, closer and closer to the sun. They were brave and strong but the god Jupiter became angry. He didn't want any mortal on Mount Olympus. Jupiter called on a gnat and made him fly in Pegasus' face. Pegasus was startled and suddenly reared up causing Bellerophon to fall off. The goddess Minerva made a soft pillow on the ground for him to fall on so he wouldn't be hurt. Pegasus flew away.

Bellerophon never rode Pegasus again. Pegasus became a beautiful legend flying forever through the skies.

Things to listen for:

Golden bridle	Pegasus galloping
Bellerophon's theme	Putting the golden bridle on Pegasus
Chimeara, the monster	Flying towards the sun
The gnat	The fall of Bellerophon
Pegasus flying away	

(Remember there are no right or wrong answers here. This is simply an exercise in listening and a means of sparking the imagination.)

Playing instructions:
    Play only on the white keys.
    Play any way you want to.

Echoes

Talk about what an echo is. Listen to the recording and try to find musical echoes.

Playing instructions:

    Play only on the white keys.

    Play any way you want to.

    Play anything you want to.

Elephant at the Circus

Listen For:

    Elephants walking

    Elephants dancing

    Dancers on the Elephants

Playing instructions:

    Play only on the white keys.

    Play any way you want to.

    Play anything you want to.

Spider and the Fly

Listen for:

    A spider

    A web

    A fly

What happens?

    Does the spider catch the fly?

    Does the fly escape?

Playing instructions:

    Play only on the white keys

    Play any way you want to.

    Play anything you want to.

Mouse Who Met a Man

This piece is about a mouse and a man who accidentally meet in the middle of the night when they both go to the same kitchen for a snack. The man jumps and frightens the mouse away, but after the man goes to sleep the mouse returns to pick up his crumbs.

Listen for:

> The story
> A clock
> The mouse
> The man

Playing instructions:

> Play only on the white keys.
> Play anything you want to.
> Play any way you want to.

Teddy Bear

Listen For:

> A Teddy Bear...
> > dancing
> > sleeping

Playing instructions:

> Play only on the black keys.
> Play anything you want to.
> Play any way you want to.

Sunset

Listen For:

> Clouds
> The sun...
> > going behind clouds
> > shining
> > sinking below the horizon
> (Listen also for the melody of "taps" interspersed throughout.)

Playing instructions:

> Play only on the white keys.
> Play anything you want to.
> Play any way you want to.

Part Two

Animals
(The introduction of the modes)

In part two of the exercises, the different harmonic languages of the modes are introduced, each with its own animal. The purpose of the animals is to provide a strong associative basis with which to identify the different colors or harmonies of each mode. In this section we also begin to move away from fists and palms, towards one hand, one finger at a time or "finger hopping."

The modes in this section are all based on the key of C, therefore, only white keys will be used. A mode is created by switching the center of the harmonic structure from one pitch to another. For example, moving the tonal center from "C" to "D" creates a whole new sound and a harmonic structure known as the dorian mode. There are seven modes for every key: In this section I introduce the first six modes of the key of C major.

Finding the primary pitch of each mode can be helpful. It's a good way to start and end an exercise (though of course there are many other possibilities and no wrong answer is possible). Study the diagram with each exercise and make a game out of locating all the primary pitches on the keyboard before playing the piece.

Once again, each of the exercises may be prepared in the following ways:
> Listen to the music.
> Dance to the music.
> Draw to the music.
> Talk about the music.

After playing all of the pieces in this section, have the child listen and attempt to identify the animal and the key of each one. Practice saying them aloud (i.e. Lion in A Natural Minor, or Horse in C Major). Try mixing up the order as well.

Horse in C Major (Ionian)

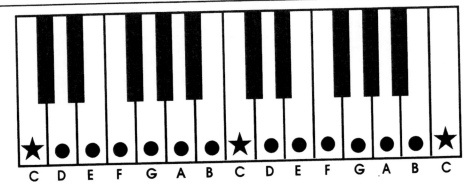

Listen For:

A Horse...
        walking
        trotting
        galloping

Playing instructions:
1. Locate all the "C's on the piano.*
2. Begin the piece by playing a "C" and try to end on a "C" as well.
3. Play only on the white keys.
4. Play anything you want to.
5. Play any way you want to but try to play with one finger at a time, part of the time.

* "C's" can be decorated with star stickers so that they are easier to locate when playing.

Dragon in D Dorian

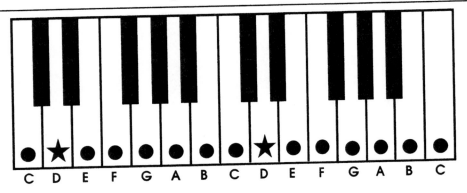

Listen For:

A Dragon...
        marching
        guarding his cave
        flying

Playing instructions:
1. Locate all the "D's" on the piano.
2. Begin the piece with a "D" and try to end on one as well.
3. Play only on the white keys.
4. Play anything you want to.
5. Play any way you want to but try to play with one finger at a time, part of the time.

Bull in E Phrygian

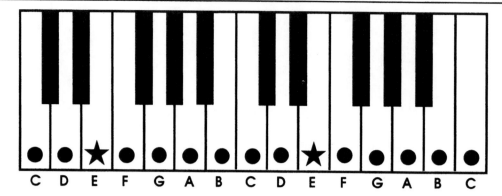

Listen For:

A Bull...

walking

eating

charging

sleeping

Playing instructions:

1. Locate all the "E's" on the piano.
2. Begin the piece with an "E" and try to end on one as well.
3. Play only on the white keys.
4. Play anything you want to.
5. Play any way you want to but try to play with one finger at a time, part of the time.

Bird in F Lydian

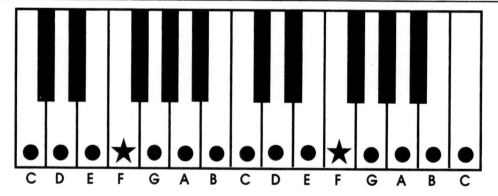

Listen For:

A Bird...

chirping

flying

hopping

Playing instructions:

1. Locate all the "F's" on the piano.
2. Begin the piece with an "F" and try to end on one as well.
3. Play only on the white keys.
4. Play anything you want to.
5. Play any way you want to but try to play with one finger at a time, part of the time.

Dolphin in G Mixolydian

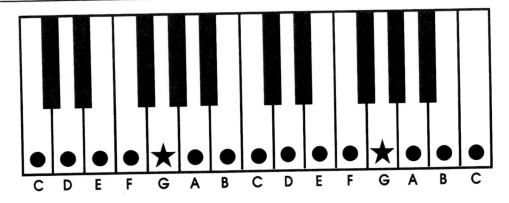

Listen For:

> The Ocean
> The Dolphin...
> > swimming under water
> > jumping out of the water

Playing instructions:

1. Locate all the "G's" on the piano.
2. Begin the piece with a "G" and try to end on one as well.
3. Play only on the white keys.
4. Play anything you want to.
5. Play any way you want to but try to play with one finger at a time, part of the time.

Lion in A Natural Minor (Aeolian)

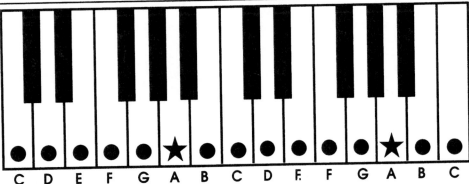

Listen For:

> The Lion
> > roaring
> > as king of the jungle
> > running

Playing instructions:

1. Locate all the "A's" on the piano.
2. Begin the piece with an "A" and try to end on one as well.
3. Play only on the white keys.
4. Play anything you want to.
5. Play any way you want to but try to play with one finger at a time, part of the time.

Part Three
Scenes

In this section the music becomes the background or accompaniment to the child's animals. Each exercise or scene has many possibilities, some of which are suggested. The child may do as many or as few as he wishes and may of course add his own animal choices.

All of these exercises use white keys exclusively. The child may choose from the following ways to play:

    1. One hand at a time, one finger at a time.
    2. Palms, fists, arms, etc.
    3. Two hands, one finger at a time.
    4. Walking fingers, one hand.
    5. Walking fingers, two hands.

The Farm

CD Track 18

Suggested animals:
    Cow
    Pig
    Horse
    Chicken
    Rooster
    Lamb
    Dog
    Cat
    Mouse

The Desert

CD Track 19

Suggested animals:
    Camel
    Vulture
    Snake

The Mountain

CD Track 20

Suggested animals:
    Eagle
    Goat
    Lion
    Coyote

The Ocean

CD Track 21

Suggested animals:
Starfish
Dolphin
Whale
Shark
Turtle
Sting Ray
Jellyfish
Flying Fish
Crab
Lobster
Seagull

The Jungle

CD Track 22

Suggested animals:
Lion
Tiger
Monkey
Parrot
Snake
Elephant

The Forest

CD Track 23

Suggested animals:
Squirrel
Chipmunk
Fox
Wolf
Bear
Deer
Snake
Sparrow
Crow
Robin
Owl

Part Four
Games

The pieces in this section can be used as games for a group of children, or as purely musical examples to do solo improvisations with. They can also be used as an alternating parent and child set.

These pieces are perhaps the most difficult because these are no extra musical ideas to rely on. They also are the most complicated technically, introducing new rules regarding question and answer phrases, cadenzas, and repeated harmonic structures. If any new rule seems too complicated or becomes frustrating to the child, simply skip it and have the child play anything he wants to on the white keys. Later, when he is ready, you can add the more complicated ideas.

Also included are games which may be used with earlier pieces, and some which do not require the recording at all. There is enough material in this section to run a class, meeting once a week, for a year. Participating in a class like this is usually very inspiring to children. They enjoy the games, but more importantly, they flourish in an environment in which their peers and parents applaud their creative ability.

This is why it is so important to review the behavioral rules of CAD at every class until they are firmly established.

#1 - "There's No Such Thing as a Mistake"

#2 - "Applause and Silence"

#3 - "Never Criticize a Friend"

If you intend to use these pieces as games with a group of children, you must read and study them all first. Be sure all parents of children in your class have read and understood this book before classes start.

"What's the Answer to My Question?"

In this exercise, there is an eight-note melody to which you can sing the words: "What's the answer to my question?"

This melody is repeated over and over in the lowest voice, forming a bass line and a repeating harmonic pattern. If the student is playing this as a solo piece, simply have him play anything he wants to on the white keys on the upper right hand side of the keyboard.

Listen For:

The "What's the answer to my question?" melody
Can you find it in a high part?
Can you find it in a low part?
Can you sing it?

To Play the Games:

Parent/Child Version:

Alternate turns, each person improvising over one or two phrases of "What's the answer to my question?"

A Group of Children:

Have the children form a line to the keyboard on the upper right hand side. Have them sing once and then take individual turns over one or two phrases of "What's the answer to my question?" It helps to have all the children continue to sing in order to help them know when it is their turn. After each turn the child goes to the end of the line. This continues until the music has ended.

An interesting and fun variation of this game is one in which the children approach the piano in pairs holding hands. They continue to hold hands as they play a duet together: one with his right hand and the other with his left. (This can also be done with parent/child pairs and is especially useful with very young or beginning classes.)

"What's the Answer to My Question?"

In this exercise, there is an eight-note melody to which you can sing the words: "What's the answer to my question?"

This is another version of the same piece and games.

Question and Answer

In this piece, the right hand (or upper voice) continually enters and drops out. The object in this game is to listen and when the hand drops out, to play. When the hand re-enters the child should stop. The teacher or parent should feel free to help the child enter and exit. (For example, a gentle tap on the shoulder when he should play or stop.)

To study this as a solo exercise, simply play anything you want on the white keys on the upper right hand side of the piano. Try to answer the melody of the recording when it drops out, and stop when it re-enters as described above.

Listen For:
The melody coming in and dropping out. (Try raising hands when it enters and dropping them when it stops.) (Try dancing when the melody enters and becoming a statue when it stops.)

To Play the Games:

Parent/Child Version
Alternate taking turns when the melody drops out.

A Group of Children:
Prepare by doing the "Listen for" exercises first. Then have the children form a line to the piano with each child getting one or two turns to answer the melody before going to the end of the line. Continue until the music ends.

Circle Cadenza

A Harmonic Minor

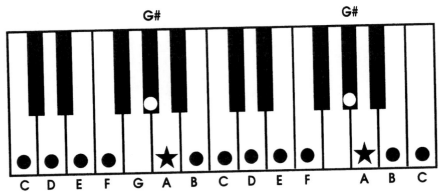

This piece is the most complicated in the book, both as a musical study and as a game. It was also voted the most fun by my former students. It is first of all challenging because it is in the key of A harmonic minor: In this key, the student may not play all the white keys; he must try not to play the note "G." (See diagram above.) As he becomes more advanced he may wish to add the one black key "G#" to the group of white keys. In order to simplify the playing in this key, the parent should mark all the "G's" with red stickers, and all the "G#'s" with green stickers so the student can easily identify them. (See diagram.)

The second reason it is challenging is that it introduces the concept of a cadenza. A cadenza is the point in a piece (usually a concerto) where the soloist plays without the orchestra, a virtuosic and freely expressive solo. In this exercise there are several points where the rhythmic regularity stops, allowing the student a great deal of freedom.

Listen For:

Cadenzas - Listen for them and raise hands when you hear one.
March to the rhythmic part and stop when a cadenza is heard.

To Play:

Solo Version:

1. Locate all the "A's" on the piano.
2. Try to begin and end the piece with this note "A."
3. Locate all the "G's." Try to avoid these notes. (They should be marked.)
4. Play using the white keys (except G).
5. Play anything you want to.
6. Play any way you want to.

Parent/Child Version:

Play in the key of A harmonic minor as described above. Play together until the cadenza part comes. One person takes a solo over the cadenza part. When the rhythmic part returns play together again. Continue by alternating solos over the cadenza part.

Group Version:

Prepare using the "listen for" games above. Be sure all the children understand the key of A harmonic minor before beginning the game.

Have the children form a circle and march when the music begins. When the cadenza part comes, whoever is in front of the piano is "caught" and gets to play a solo. When the march returns the soloist continues to play and the other students (who stopped for the cadenza) resume marching. When the next cadenza comes, another student is caught and the first player is seated in the middle of the circle. This continues until all the children have had a turn.

Part Five

More Games

Guessing Games

I began using guessing games to encourage the children to listen to each other in a fun way. I soon realized that the children could get a lot more out of listening then I imagined. Their ability to hear and determine modes aurally, to imagine animals and scenes musically, and to create and communicate these things to each other is amazing.

Game One: Animals with Matching Modes

The point of this game is to learn how to aurally identify six modes by hearing them in conjunction with a matching animal (i.e. Lion in A natural minor, or a Horse in C major etc.). Use the six modes and music of Part Two of the recording. One at a time have the children come to the piano and choose one of the six animals in Part Two (Horse, Dragon, Lion, Bull, Bird, or Dolphin). Have him perform his choice with the recording. After applauding, allow the listening children to guess what the animal and key was. (I always allow all the children to guess before telling the answer.) In the beginning you will have to remind them of the possible answers and the accompanying modes. Have them repeat the names of the modes and animals after you to help them learn them. After they have played this game for several weeks they can begin to identify the piece solely by its mode.

Suggestion:

If you can find a set of small animal figures or pictures to remind the children of the possibilities, or to choose from when they come to the piano, this can be a fun way to develop their abilities faster. Also, have the listening children act out or dance the animal they think is being played occasionally, for fun and to help keep them from getting restless.

Game Two: Creating Animals

Using the music from "Part Three: Scenes" have the children create their own animals for the given scene. This opens up many creative possibilities and is therefore harder than the previous game. Play this as in the first guessing game, each child taking a turn playing while the others try to guess. Those guessing may try to guess the scene (i.e. Forest, Mountain, etc.), the animal, or both at the teacher's discretion.

Toy Bag:

Sometimes the possible animals seem endless to the guessers and a toy bag becomes helpful. Have a group of animal figures for each scene. Let the performing child pick one out of the scene he wishes to play and return it to the collection. Allow the other children to look at the collection while the performance is going on. (This is also a good way to diversify a child who continually picks the same animal over and over.)

Multiple Players:

Have two children perform together each playing the same animal, or each playing their own animal (i.e. one is a cat and the other is a mouse). Children can also guess in pairs or teams which makes it more fun. Allow them time at the end of the performance to discuss and come up with an answer. Do not allow them to discuss the answer during the performance: remind them of the applause and silence rule.

Silent Ear Training

A silent ear is the ear which listens to the imagination. It is the ear which can hear a melody or harmony that only exists in the mind. It is like the ability to read silently; one looks at the page and reads the words but no sound is produced to anyone else.

It is very important to develop this "silent ear" for several reasons. Number one being that it is the way the subconscious communicates to the conscious part of the brain. Number two, using this silent ear to create music stimulates the subconscious to a much higher level because it requires much greater concentration then regular improvisation does.

Preparation:

Game One:
Play a note on the piano. Ask the children to close their eyes and raise their hands when they can no longer hear it. When all the hands are raised repeat the game and ask them to listen harder. When all the hands are up, tell them that you can still hear it. Have them try to hear it, then try to sing it. After they have done this, explain that though the note was actually gone it went someplace else. It went into their inner ear, or inside their heads. Repeat the listening again and this time when the note has disappeared, have them try to sing it.

Game Two:
Play a note until it is completely gone. Have the children sing it. Have them try to sing it silently in their heads. Play some different notes while they concentrate on the first one. Have them try to sing the original note again out loud. (Suggestion: Start this game using only black keys, after a few weeks try using only white keys.)

Note:
It takes a while for children to be able to do this. Do not be disappointed if the pitches do not match. Just practicing the exercise is developing their silent ear ability.

Creative Silent Ear Games:
1. Choose any piece from the tape. Have the children sit quietly and try to imagine a melody silently.

2. Repeat the above, but then ask if anyone thought of anything. If no one did (a strong possibility) then have each child come up and play a solo to the chosen piece while the others continue to try to imagine one. After this repeat the silent creative exercise without anyone playing. Again ask if any one thought of a melody. If yes, have those children come up and try to play what they thought of.

Note:
It takes a while for children to be able to do this. They are often uncomfortable trying to play what they thought of because they are afraid of forgetting it or being unable to reproduce it. Be encouraging but don't force. Explain that you don't expect them to remember it exactly, nor do you or anyone else know what they imagined. Therefore, nobody is judging them and "there's no such thing as a mistake." Eventually all the children should be encouraged to play even if they didn't imagine anything. Explain to those who do not imagine anything, that one has to hear and create a lot of music first before the silent ear will work.

Hint: A good first choice is "What's the Answer to My Question?" because of the repeating bass line.

Games Without the Recording

Clapping Games

There are several purposes of the clapping games: One, to break down barriers of self-consciousness; two, to begin the process of sharing ideas; three, to begin to create rhythmic ideas; four, to stress the importance of rhythmic creation; and five, to help create a warm, fun and friendly environment within which to create. For these reasons, I often start a new group with a clapping game.

A good basic one to start with is a group imitation of a solo creation. Have the group sit in a circle. The teacher claps a short rhythm using hands and knees, floor, stomach, head, etc. The class then repeats back the rhythm with the teacher leading. Ask who wants to make up the next one. Allow as many children to create and lead one as wish to. Don't push those who are not ready.

Often students will try all kinds of silly expressions and sounds, to experiment and also sometimes to test the "no such thing as a mistake" rule. I allow these expressions as long as they are not rude or disruptive to the class. I find that my allowance and participation in the silliness often serves as a means of removing the remnants of self-consciousness from the class.

Variations:

Silent Clapping Game:
Play like the basic game but make no sound (i.e. hit lightly). This is a great one for bringing order to an unruly group.

Pass a Clap:
Sit in a circle. Have one person start a rhythm. Have each player try to do what the person next to him did (not the original player). If he can't do it, he can either say "pass," or make up a new rhythm. The point of this exercise is communication.

This game can also be played silently by holding hands. One person begins by gently squeezing a rhythm into the hand of the person next to him. It is then passed around the circle ending with the originator. Remember "There's no such thing as a mistake."

Non-Imitative Circle:
Sit in a circle. Have each player take a turn creating his own rhythm. The object of this game is to try not to do what someone else did!

Elbows, Palms, and Fingers

Clapping games lead easily into this game. Its purpose is primarily to break down inhibitions regarding the piano and creating in general.

To Play:
Seat three or four children at a piano. The first child is asked to play anything he wants to with two stipulations: One, it should be short, and two he may only play with his elbows. Each of the other students is asked to imitate the first, again using only elbows.

Repeat the process using palms, and then finally fingers. White or black keys should be chosen for each set of elbows, palms and fingers.

All the children should have a chance to be the leader as well as a follower.

The "It" Game in F# Pentatonic

"It" is a tapper. The game is something like a musical game of tag. In the beginning the teacher should be the tapper. Later the children can take turns.

Three players sit at the piano. The rest form a line to the piano. "It" taps the players four times:

One	-	Start to play
Two	-	Stop
Three	-	Start to play
Four	-	Leave the piano

When one of the players leaves the piano a new one sits down. This continues until all the students have had a turn. Use only black keys for this game.

Note: The "It" game could be played with any of the pieces on the recording by following the specified keys (i.e. white or black).

Rhythm/Instrument Duet or Trio

One student is given a drum. A toy drum works great. If one is not available create one out of material at hand (i.e. spoons on a pot). The student creates a rhythm on his drum. A second student sits at the piano and creates a melody. When they are finished they trade places.

More than one player can play the drums and more than one player can play the piano. The only rules for multiple players are: One, enter one at a time and two, choose the key ahead of time (i.e. black keys or white keys only).

A One Pitch Piece

The purpose of this exercise is to study all the non-pitch elements of music. We often get bogged down trying to create melody and harmony and forget all the other great elements. To play this game instruct the students to create a song out of one note. This is difficult so it will help to demonstrate. Here are some possible elements to explore:

Dynamics: Variations of loud and soft
Tempo: Changing the speed of the pulse
Rhythm: Variations of the speed of individual notes
Articulation: Variations on how the note is hit short, long, hard, gentle
Expression: Changing the mood of the note (i.e. angry, sad, happy, funny, silly)

Structuring A Group Class

In order to work with a group of two-to five-year-olds, organization and structure is necessary. The following ideas are designed to aid in both keeping order and control of the class, and creating a good learning environment.

Blankets

Have each student bring a blanket to sit on. Any old crib blanket or soft towel will do. This provides him with comfort as well as a defined place in the room. The rule should be that the student is always on his blanket when not instructed to be elsewhere. Additional emotional security is provided by the parent who sits on the blanket or directly behind the child.

Rules

The three rules of CAD should be clearly spelled out before each class begins until they are firmly established.

#1 - "There's No Such Thing as a Mistake"

#2 - "Applause and Silence"

#3 - "Never Criticize a Friend"

Length

A good beginning class length is about a half hour. As the attention span and behavior mature that can be lengthened to an hour. Five to eight children per class should be the maximum unless they are all five-to six-year-olds.

Group and Solo Mix

There should be a mixture of group and solo work. Young children need lots of variation. It is hard for them to listen for long periods of time. They also need to move, so some movement games interspersed is a good idea. Solo work should be done weekly so the students become comfortable creating and performing for each other.

Repetition and Variation

Repetition of a creative exercise is the key to the development of creative ability. Therefore, certain games should be repeated on a weekly basis.

> #1 - What's the Answer to My Question?
> #2 - Silent Ear Training
> #3 - Clapping Games
> #4 - Question and Answer
> #5 - Circle Cadenza

These are all good choices, but they do not all need to be in every class. For example, #1 could be repeated for the first month, then add #2, etc.

Variation sparks new ideas and triggers creativity. Therefore, new games or games which are constantly changing are also important (i.e. animal guessing games).

A Typical Class

A typical class would follow something like this:

> #1 - Students on Blankets
> #2 - Review the Rules
> #3 - Clapping Games
> #4 - Animal Guessing Games
> #5 - What's the Answer to My Question?
> #6 - A New Game - (i.e. Rhythm/Duet)

Behavior Problems

Often there are one or two children who cannot sit still or take an instruction. This usually means they are not ready for a class yet. They may be too young. You may include them as observers, or if they are too disruptive, have them wait a year. They may be able to work in a one-on-one situation with a parent or teacher in the meantime.

Performance

It is good to periodically have a CAD concert. It gives the children a big boost of confidence to perform and receive applause from their parents and peers. Be sure however that your audience understands the concept of equal praise for all children.

A concert should include solos as well as group pieces. Solos should be prepared by practice at home starting at least two weeks prior to the concert. Each child should choose a different piece from the recording to practice daily.

Group pieces can include anything practiced during the year. For example:

What's the Answer to My Question?
A Harmonic Minor Circle Cadenza
Question and Answer

Don't forget to have a party after to celebrate!

A Final Word - "Fun"

Perhaps the single most important element in having a successful creative experience is having fun.

Having fun...

> relaxes a student
> frees inhibitions
> allows creative exploration
> encourages willing repetition
> encourages positive relationships
> encourages open creative communication
> builds self-confidence
> builds willing self-criticism
> develops performance ability

among other things...

And having fun is simple. There is no criticism; there is applause; there is respect and there is friendship if all the rules are followed. Further, there are lots of games to play: once the basics are established, let the children choose the games. Let them be silly (within reason, of course) and you be silly too. Have concerts and parties to celebrate the students' development. Above all, respect each child. Respect his wonderful beginning creative ability, respect his need to participate when ready, respect his need to communicate what he's feeling, respect each child's self-critical search for truth and beauty. He will find it!

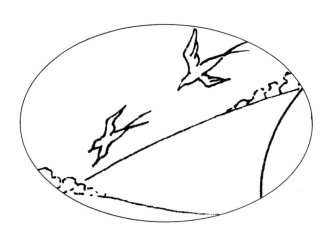